FOR EVERY CAUSE?

The Question of Divorce

For Every Cause?

The Question of Divorce

John Williams

EXETER
THE PATERNOSTER PRESS

NEPTUNE, NEW JERSEY
LOIZEAUX BROTHERS

AUSTRALIA:
*Bookhouse Australia Ltd.,
PO Box 115, Flemington Markets, NSW 2129*

SOUTH AFRICA:
*Oxford University Press,
PO Box 1141, Cape Town*

British Library Cataloguing in Publication Data

Williams, John
  For every cause?
  1. Divorce—Biblical teaching
  I. Title
  220.8'30689   BS680.D/

ISBN 0-85364-330-X

Library of Congress Cataloging in Publication Data

Williams, John, 1928—Nov.23—
  For every cause?

  Bibliography, p.96
  Index included.
    1. Divorce—Religious aspects—Christianity.
  2. Remarriage—Religious aspects—Christianity.
  3. Divorce—Biblical teaching. 4. Remarriage—
  Biblical teaching.   I. Title.
  BV835.W544 1982   241'.63   82-158
  ISBN 0-87213-953-0   AACR2

*Typeset in 11/12 Century Schoolbook by
Nuprint Services Ltd., Harpenden, Hertfordshire*

*Printed in Great Britain for the Publishers
by A. Wheaton & Co. Ltd., Exeter.*

Contents

DEDICATED
TO MY BELOVED WIFE,
AUDREY

Proverbs 31:28

Preface

Divorce has touched the life or family of almost everyone we know. In fact it has reached epidemic proportions and is exerting extreme pressures on society in general, as well as on the church. As Christians, many of us feel we should do something but we are not altogether clear what. Surely the first thing we must do is discover what God has to say on the matter and then attempt to think about ways in which we can practically and courageously apply God's word in love.

Of course anyone who reads the Bible carefully will quickly discover there are no pat, easy answers to the problem of divorce. Indeed, faced with the confusion and complexity of some of our contemporary marital madnesses, there sometimes appear to be no specific answers in the Bible – certainly not the "chapter and verse" variety some folk crave!

However, far from deterring us, this lack of specific instruction may well stimulate us to seek out carefully those clear biblical principles that have to do with human relationships. As we study these we must keep in mind two things. First, people are more important than religious rules and regulations, and second, God's love for fallen man is as unvarying as his righteous standards.

When we discuss with our Christian friends such delicate subjects as divorce, or remarriage after divorce, we shall encounter all kinds of diverse and even strange points of view. For example, there will be the well-meaning minority (hopefully!) whose attitude will be: Well, if people make themselves hard beds, they should lie on them. After all, the church is in the business of saving souls not interfering in people's marriages and families! There will be other Christians who like the proverbial ostrich will bury their saintly heads in the sand and hope that such "messy matters" as divorce will go away. Unfortunately such problems do not go away. In fact it might be kind to warn the would-be ostriches that it is already too late, that head-burying leaves one very visible and very vulnerable!

Some people will assert that unless you have personally experienced divorce you cannot possibly understand the problem nor feel for those whose marriages have been shipwrecked.

10

Fortunately, this is not true; anymore than it is true to say that only those who have experienced drowning can appreciate the terrible plight of the man who has fallen overboard without a life jacket! Undoubtedly there are deep hurts and resentments that are understood better by those who have experienced the pain of divorce. However, there are many genuinely concerned people who although not divorced, are anxious to reach out the hand of Christian love and concern.

In concluding this brief preface let us plead for tolerance and understanding. Certainly we make no claim either to treat the subject of divorce exhastively nor to have discovered all the answers. We have found in this matter as in many, it is easier to legislate than to love. There is much wisdom in the words of a godly, Bible teacher of an earlier generation, who wrote:

> There is shown in the word of God a principle of divine toleration of evils that cannot be completely cured because of existing conditions. The ideal ought indeed to be striven after. God aims at it, men ought to do so. But until this can be attained God tolerates much that is as yet irremovable. Walking on the lower level does indeed involve its due recompense of reward, but the full penal consequences are not always enforced.
> (G. H. Lang, writing in an unpublished paper on "Divorce and Re-marriage according to the Scriptures.")

11

We send forth these pages in the prayerful hope that all who read them will be helped to a better understanding of God's Word and a deeper experience of his love. Remember, the same God who said through Malachi: "I hate divorce", also said through Hosea (whose partner had been blatantly immoral), I will heal their wayward-ness and love them freely, for my anger is turned away from them. (cp. Malachi 2:16 and Hosea 14:4 NIV).

Vancouver, B. C.
July 1980.

(The Bible quotations at the head of each chapter are from the New International Version, *published by Hodder and Stoughton Ltd.,* © *1978 by the New York International Bible Society.)*

CHAPTER ONE

Problems and Criteria

*Your Word is a lamp to my feet and a light for my path
(Psalm 119:105).*

Today, we are faced with a seemingly impossible
and deteriorating situation in the area of
marriage and divorce. In North America for
example, there are almost as many divorces and
separations as there are new marriages every
year. Obviously such a state of affairs constitutes
what may well be described as our greatest
sociological problem. The magnitude of the problem becomes more apparent if we remember that
the dissolution of a couple's marriage has many
"spin-offs", especially as it affects the lives of
children, relations and friends. It involves real
estate, property ownership, legal contracts,
affiliations and a hundred and one other things.
Divorce is never a simple thing but a complexity
of domestic, personal, psychological, physical,
material, financial and spiritual involvements.

13

Obviously the church will be involved in the problem of divorce. After all, most marriages, are still "solemnized" before a minister of the church. Quite apart from the church's part in initiating most marriages, it also bears a responsibility to speak on social issues such as divorce. Furthermore, it is the church that must seek to help people who are the hurt and alienated victims of a divorce. This may mean one or both of the partners of the marriage which is being dissolved, or the offspring.

Besides accepting this kind of helping role, the Christian Church must face up to the necessity of speaking on the basic issues of marriage and family. We are faced not only with this moral responsibility but also with the practical issue of our relationship to the divorced. For example, is divorce ever permissible as far as the church is concerned? If so, then on what grounds? Perhaps even more basic, what are our criteria? If we opt for the position that divorce should never be countenanced, does this mean we are willing to refuse membership in the church to at least half the total number of our contemporary, adult society – i.e. those who have been or are party to a divorce? Even if we take the position that divorce is not a question which involves church membership, we must still know whether the church should remarry people who have been divorced. The problem is two-fold. If on the one hand we support a conservative position which both disallows divorce and refuses to be involved in the remarriage of divorced people, then we take a stance which will inevitably alienate the church from our society. Worse, we may discover that we are taking a position different from that taken by Christ and the writers of Scripture. On the other hand, if we seek to liberalize our divorce teaching or even accept the modern "do-it-yourself", "let's-get-it-over" approach, we stand in grave danger of espousing such a low view of marriage that we end up abetting the erosion of the family, if not society itself.

It is never easy to decide issues in human behaviour. It is particularly complex when that behaviour affects other people and even human society at its very roots. However, we must not be deterred by the difficulty nor must we look for easy ways out of the dilemma such as pretending we are not involved. It seems like moral cowardice for a particular church to adopt the position that while it will not marry divorced persons, it will recognize their remarriage if performed by the minister of another church. This implies that such a church then welcomes the couple into membership, once they are remarried. Could it be that it is more interested in money than in sense?

For the purpose of this booklet we shall take the position that the consistent, self-revelation of God and his will in Scripture is our final criterion. Church practice and precedent, not to mention tradition, may be helpful and will be wisely considered, but they are not authoritative. The norm is the Word of God. Having said this we must recognize two or three other things. Firstly, we believe that the Bible in all its parts is a consistent unity. There is not one view of marriage and divorce which might be described as "Jewish" or "Old Testament", and another which might be called "Christian". Development and progressive revelation there may be, but patent conflict and contradiction between the various parts of Scripture there will not be. Secondly, we must be at least as zealous to discern and act in the true spirit of Scripture as to understand its literal statements. In this as in everything, it is the Spirit that gives life, the letter can be deadly. Thirdly, we must admit that it is much easier to offer theological opinions and ethical decrees from the "cloister", than to give practical help and encouragement to people as they are struggling in the dust and heat of life. Certainly the church must speak out against sin, and resist all attempts to temporize or accommodate the Word of God. However, she must recognize herself to be a community of forgiven sinners whose task is to win men from their sin to Christ. Her primary task is evangelism not casuistry.

CHAPTER TWO

Moses' Bill of Divorcement

*Do not let this Book of the Law depart from your
mouth; meditate on it day and night, so that you may
be careful to do everything written in it
(Joshua 1:8).*

When Jesus discussed divorce with the Jewish
leaders of his day, reference was made to a particular Old Testament passage.

> When a man hath taken a wife, and married her,
> and it come to pass that she find no favour in his
> eyes because he hath found some uncleaness in
> her; then let him write her a bill of divorcement,
> and give it in her hand, and send her out of his
> house. And when she is departed out of his house,
> she may go and be another man's wife (Deute-
> ronomy 24:1–2).

There are two points to be noted here. Firstly,
divorce was allowed under the Mosaic law on the

basis of the discovery of "uncleanness". Secondly, this divorce evidently so completely severed the marriage bond that the "unclean" spouse was free to remarry. This is very important for our discussion because it demonstrates that divorce in the Mosaic economy, as indeed in Jewish thought generally, was not merely separation *a thoro et mensa* (from bed and table) to use the ancient patristic formula, but complete dissolution of the marriage (i.e. *a vinculo matrimonii* – from the bonds of marriage). Several other things emerge from the context of this Deuteronomic legislation. One is that the Mosaic law not only allowed for remarriage after divorce, but even for another marriage after a second divorce. The only exception to this third marriage was that the divorcee might not remarry her former husband (Deuteronomy 24:4). Such legislation may seem quite "liberal" in our thinking but we must examine the facts more closely.

Another thing seems obvious from the earlier part of this context. In Deuteronomy 22:21–24 and Leviticus 10:10, we see that immorality was punished by stoning whether the party to the immorality was married or simply betrothed. This harsher legislation which was intended to "put away evil from Israel", makes one thing abundantly clear, that is, that the "uncleanness" referred to as a ground for divorce in Deuteronomy 24:1, was something different from extra-marital intercourse. This is obvious since, if a husband discovered his wife to be immoral, he had her executed. He did not give her a bill of divorcement so that she could go off and marry her paramour!

What then we must ask, constituted "uncleanness"? The Hebrew word *ervah-dabhar* is translated in various ways. Gesenius, the famous Hebraist, suggests "indecency" or "improper behaviour". Edersheim says that the word might include any impropriety, appearance of loose-living, fraud before marriage or indecency. Our modern English versions translate it "something shameful" (NEB, RSV, Ampl., NAS). The NIV reads rather ambiguously, "something indecent about her". Later Jewish casuistry used this word "uncleanness" as an excuse for all manner of trivial grounds for divorce. For example, poor management, poor cooking or even homeliness (in the North American sense) were considered grounds for divorce by some of the Jewish rabbis.

Such permissiveness must surely be viewed as a travesty of the Mosaic legislation. The divorce provision was obviously intended as a protection both of the sanctity of marriage and of a wife who might be the unhappy victim of a cruel husband's anger or insinuation. Neither in this particular biblical context nor any other is divorce suggested as a necessity or as a divine ideal. Restoration and reconciliation are better than dissolution. Divorce is always an accommodation to the sinfulness and failure of man to live as God intended. Divorce was given as a limit not a permit. The beautiful yet pathetic story of the book of Hosea teaches that men, like God, can forgive even the most blatant moral offence.

Before examining the New Testament teaching on the subject of divorce, we must take time to consider God's original ideal in marriage. This ideal is clearly stated in Genesis 2:24.

> Therefore shall a man leave his father and mother, and shall cleave unto his wife: and they shall be one flesh.

There are many important implications here and all have a bearing on our present topic. First and foremost, it is obvious that in God's order in creation, his plan was one man for one woman. To cite the Bible in support of polygamy is thoroughly to misconstrue its plain intent and teaching. Whenever men forsook monogamy for polygamy, no matter how famous or spiritual they might have been, they departed from the divine ideal and involved themselves and posterity in endless trouble (cf. Genesis 16).

In the Genesis account of man's creation, man and woman are viewed as complementary to each other. They are so to speak, two halves of one whole. Though distinct and different in themselves, they are part of, and for, each other. Woman, (*isshah*) was taken out of man (*ish*) and yet she was brought to man in the divine arithmetic of marriage which is $1+1=1$. The union of man and woman in this story involved two distinct processes. On the one hand there was the "leaving", and on the other the "cleaving".

These two processes of leaving and cleaving are still essential to the true experience of marriage. The partners are prepared for marriage as members of two distinct family units which they did not choose. They were born unto those separate families and have existed as representative and integral parts of them. Now they come to a totally new and different mode of existence. They are married to each other as husband and wife. By their union they not only become "one flesh", which, while involving physical union appears to include much more, but they establish a new entity – a family unit.

The same permanence which characterized their physical relationship with their separate families should now characterize their chosen relationship with each other. Unfortunately, as we know only too well, this beautiful relationship is not indissoluble only by death. There is such a thing as divorce and under certain tragic circumstances even the Bible allows for this, as we shall see.

CHAPTER THREE

Jesus' Teaching about Divorce

Moses permitted you to divorce your wives because your hearts were hard. But it was not this way from the beginning
(Matthew 19:8–9).

Our Lord's teaching regarding the subject of divorce is found in the three Synoptic gospels. The references are as follows: 1. Matthew 5:31–32; 2. Matthew 19:3–12; 3. Mark 10:2–12; 4. Luke 16:18.

1. Context

In the first of these passages which is part of the Sermon on the Mount, Jesus is contrasting his teaching about divorce with the traditional rabbinical view of the subject: The traditional view which Jesus cites,

> Whosoever shall put away his wife let him give her a writing of divorcement. (Greek: apostasion)

smacks of an attempt to water down what the Deuteronomic text actually said. Notice there is no reference here to the clause, "discovery of uncleanness", found in the Mosaic legislation. The Scribes and Pharisees were looking no doubt, for a popular, "easy out" theory of escape from the marriage contract. In contrast, the Lord says:

> but I say unto you that whosoever shall put away his wife, saving for fornication causeth her to commit adultery: and whosoever shall marry her that is divorced committeth adultery.

Far from accepting the traditional, easy option for divorce, Jesus here teaches that a man who divorces his wife is guilty on two counts. On the one hand he causes his wife to commit adultery. This presupposes that she will remarry (a possible course open to a divorcee on the basis of both scripture and Jewish tradition), or be forced through dire necessity into prostitution. On the other hand he causes her next marriage partner to commit adultery as well. This is because this man is "becoming one flesh" with a woman who is still in God's sight, one flesh with her husband. The only extenuating circumstance allowed by Jesus is "fornication" (*porneia*). We shall discuss this exception later. The Lucan passage is similar to the Matthean although it makes the husband who initiates the divorce as well as his second wife, the offenders, rather than the wife who is put away. Luke also omits the excepting clause. The two Synoptic passages which deal with divorce at length are Matthew 19:3–12 and Mark 10:2–12. These are parallel accounts of Jesus' conversation with the Pharisees who had come to question him about the legality of Moses' divorce law. There were, among the Pharisees, two schools of thought about divorce. On the one hand those who followed Hillel advocated a lax attitude and taught that a man could divorce his wife "for any cause". On the other, the Pharisees who followed the more conservative Rabbi Shammai, taught that there was only one ground for divorce, that was, fornication. The Pharisees who challenged Jesus about this whole issue may have been surprised to discover that his opinion aligned more closely with Shammai's.

As we compare the Matthean and Marcan accounts of Jesus' words we discover they are practically identical. However, Matthew has some additions and we must consider these. For example the wording of the question put to Jesus reads in Matthew:

Is it lawful for a man to put away his wife for every cause? (for any and every reason NIV)

Whereas in Mark, the words "for every cause" are omitted. Secondly, and this is the more famous variant, Mark reads simply:

25

Whosoever shall put away his wife, and marry another, committeth adultery....

while Matthew has,

Whosoever shall put away his wife, except it be for fornication (porneia), and shall marry another committeth adultery....

The third, additional section reported by Matthew is Jesus' words about eunuchs. Before discussing the famous "excepting clause" let us notice the whole thrust of Jesus' reply to the Pharisees, as reported by both Evangelists. The Pharisees, probably followers of Shammai, wanted Jesus to do two things. Firstly, they wanted him to give public support to their viewpoint, and secondly, they hoped he would cast doubt on the lawfulness of the more liberal contention that a man could obtain a divorce on any grounds. Although Jesus' view was in line with that of Shammai, he skilfully refused to be cast in the role of supporting any particular school of thought. Instead of being drawn into a debate about the lawfulness of this or that opinion, he went behind the Mosaic legislation about divorce, right back to God's order in creation. God's ideal, according to Jesus, did not even envisage divorce. It simply had to do with a man and a woman being joined together as one, in the pristine purity of a world without sin. Jesus

26

would talk about divorce, but first he wanted his hearers to recall the loveliness of marriage as God intended it. Only against that beautiful backdrop could the ugliness and tragedy of sin and all its concomitants like divorce, be properly observed. God's plan was for the man and woman to be "joined together". Man's interest seemed to be in "putting them asunder", and this, said Jesus, was not man's business.

2. The "Excepting Clause"

Despite opinions to the contrary, there is no dependable manuscript evidence for omitting Jesus' "excepting clause" from the text of Matthew's Gospel. Textually the matter is settled. However we may explain the difference between the texts of Matthew and Mark, at least we cannot do so on the grounds of textual manipulation.

Various suggestions are made and we must briefly consider them. Most New Testament scholars tend to accept the priority of the Marcan text. While Mark offers the shortest account of the life and teaching of Jesus, he sometimes gives a fuller version of incidents than Matthew or Luke. Certainly we must allow that our doctrine of biblical inspiration does not require that the story of Jesus be reported in identical words by each of the Evangelists. Peter's explanation of inspiration seems useful here. He wrote:

Men spake from God as they were borne along by the Holy Ghost (2 Peter 1:21).

Obviously, Peter is here referring to Old Testament writers, but for him it would be equally true of the New Testament writers. (For example, he attributes inspiration to Paul in 2 Peter 3:16.) In other words the Holy Spirit used real, live men, men of their own times and circumstances, to write down the Word of God in their peculiar styles and idioms. He did not use automata or teleprinters, but people like us. Though as liable to sin and error as we, they were preserved in their special task of writing inerrant scripture, through the gracious providence of the Holy Spirit.

Thus it is that we have four different Gospels. Quite apart from their interaction and use of common oral tradition or common written source documents, they provide us with a four-point compass look at the eternal Christ now manifested in flesh, for us men and our salvation. We need all four Gospels to give us a picture of Christ in true perspective.

Without embarking on a discussion of the Synoptic problem, it must be evident to the careful reader that Matthew tends to give the more expanded account of our Lord's life. He includes considerable portions of Jesus' discourses and teaching, over sixty paragraphs, which are peculiar to him. Against this background we can understand that whereas Mark gives us précis of Jesus' teaching on divorce, Matthew gives us the fuller account. To put it another way, Mark gives us the general principle enunciated by Jesus; that is, that marriage is to be regarded as a sacred institution of permanent validity. Matthew on the other hand deals with a particular situation in which Jesus, while retaining his high view of marriage, and understanding the hardness of the human heart, recognizes divorce as a possible accommodation for sinful, human beings.

At the heart of our Lord's excepting clause is the word "fornication", which translates the Greek, *porneia*. There is considerable discussion as to Jesus' exact meaning when he used this word. Noting that the excepting clause occurs only in Matthew, the Gospel especially slanted to Jewish readers, some suggest that *porneia* might mean consanguineous marriage (i.e. marriage between blood relations) such as is proscribed by Leviticus 18. However, since such marriage would be considered incestuous and was forbidden to Jews, it would therefore be a rarity in their society. Thus it is unlikely that Jesus meant this. Furthermore this sort of act might well come under the heading of "fraud", along with things like the deliberate concealment of mental illness, impotency, or another marriage. In this case it would not be a question of divorce, but annulment. The marriage should never have taken place.

A further suggestion is that we should understand Jesus' reference is to premarital sin.
However, practically all our lexicographical
evidence demonstrates that we cannot establish
a linguistic case for translating *porneia* in this
narrow sense. In fact the evidence is quite to the
contrary and we are safe in assuming that
porneia and *zanah* (its Hebrew equivalent) are
frequently used synonymously along with
"adultery" (*moicheia*) in Scripture. (In his article
under *PORNEIA*, Vine writes: "...is used of illicit
sexual intercourse...in Matthew 5:32 and 19:9
it stands for, or includes, adultery" – *Expository
Dictionary of New Testament*, Vol. II p.125.) In
passing we might again remind ourselves that a
person who engaged in pre-marital sex was
summarily dealt with by Judaism. He was
executed (Deuteronomy 22:22). There are no
divorce suits hereafter! We shall be safe in
assuming that by his use of the strong, compre-
hensive term *porneia*, Jesus meant that every
kind of sexual sin, perversion or promiscuity
might be conceded as grounds for divorce. He is
maximizing rather than minimizing the seriousness of sin. The NIV translates Jesus' words:
"except for marital unfaithfulness". Having said
this, we must be fair to the text and notice that
while divorce may be conceded on these grounds,
it is still not commanded or required. This was
true, according to Jesus, also under the Mosaic

legislation. Notice his careful language, "Moses allowed (*epetrepsen*) you to put away your wife."

We might also offer the further caveat, that while refusing a too narrow interpretation for *porneia* we must also refuse a too liberal one! After all, *porneia* cannot possibly be stretched to mean "incompatibility" and the like. Otherwise we are back to the "any cause" argument of Hillel which Jesus unequivocally rejects.

Before proceeding to an examination of Paul's teaching on this subject there are two other questions we must face.

(a) *Is there a contradiction between the teaching of Jesus and that of Moses on the subject of divorce?* None whatsoever! If Moses had said, as the Pharisees implied by their trick questions (v. 3 and v. 7), that the Law commanded a man to give his wife a bill of divorcement for any cause whatsoever, there would be discrepancy. As it is, Moses neither 'commanded' divorce nor did he permit it, except for uncleanness, which the margin renders "matter of nakedness". Accepting as we do, the unity and consistency of scripture, we submit that Jesus was interpreting and elucidating Moses' words particularly for the sake of his followers. Little wonder his disciples considered his teaching strict, if not practically impossible of attainment. Jesus' standards were and still are high, and only through his grace in regeneration can we offer him obedience.

(b) *If we accept the interpretation of* porneia,

31

suggested above (i.e. that it meant extra-marital sin,) then how do we account for the attitude of Joseph the husband of Mary, the mother of Jesus? We read in Matthew 1:19,

> Because Joseph her husband was a righteous man and did not want to expose her to public disgrace, he had in mind to divorce her quietly.

Although Joseph is here described as Mary's husband, it is quite evident from the angelic message purposely given to him to allay his fears (v. 20), that he was in reality only Mary's fiancé. This is confirmed in the more intimate nativity narrative of Dr. Luke (cf. Luke 1:35, 2:5). Joseph and Mary were evidently betrothed, or as we would say, "engaged" and under Jewish law a betrothal was such a solemn contract that it was practically tantamount to marriage. This is evident from the words of Deuteronomy 22:24. If a man sexually assaulted a woman who was betrothed to another man he was considered to have committed a capital offence. He died because he had violated another man's "wife". If the betrothed woman acquiesced in the immoral act, she too died.

The only way a Jewish betrothal might be dissolved was evidently by a properly drawn up divorce. This explains Joseph's intention upon his discovery of Mary's pregnancy. Faced with this enigma, as a righteous man, Joseph felt obliged to divorce Mary but in order to spare her feelings and shield her from public scandal he decided to act with discretion and privacy. It must have been a tremendous relief to Joseph to receive the angelic explanation of Mary's condition. We may note in passing, that Joseph's attitude in this situation is worthy of more consideration than it is usually afforded. First of all he must have been thoroughly convinced of Mary's integrity and innocence, otherwise he would have considered not divorce but execution. This incidentally disposes of the argument offered by some sceptical commentators who deny the supernatural element in the story of the Incarnation. They suggest that the doctrine of the Virgin Birth was an attempt to cover Jesus' illegitimacy. Of course there are hints that Jesus had to live with this kind of vicious insinuation, while he was here on earth (John 8:41).

Secondly, Joseph the upright must have been a man of great faith. Not only did he unquestioningly accept the supernatural nature of Mary's pregnancy, but delayed consummating his marriage until after the birth of the baby Jesus (Matthew 1:24–25). We cannot imagine how steadfast Joseph's faith must have been, especially in the light of the insinuations and innuendos he no doubt had to live with in the bazaars and in the carpenter's workshop at Nazareth. His faith not only survived these assaults but supported him as he tenderly cared

for Mary during the months of her confinement,
and then for both Mary and her holy babe in the
ongoing years.

CHAPTER FOUR

Paul's Teaching

*God has called us to peace
(1 Corinthians 7:15).*

Paul's teaching about marriage, while occuring
incidentally throughout his epistles, is largely
confined to two passages: Ephesians 5 and
1 Corinthians 7. It is obvious that the Apostle
entertains the same high view of the sanctity
and permanence of marriage as his Master and
as the other writers of Scripture.

1. New Problems

The subject of divorce is discussed by Paul in
1 Corinthians 7. There, no doubt in answer to
questions raised by members of the Church in
Corinth, the Apostle offers guidelines for various
specific situations. In order to appreciate Paul's
emphasis in this chapter, we must recognize
several things. Firstly, Paul is facing different

situations from those envisaged either in the Deuteronomic code or in the teaching of Jesus. He is offering advice to Christians who come from various ethnic, cultural and religious backgrounds. Some of them find themselves in mixed marriage situations, in the sense that one partner is a Christian believer, the other is not.

Secondly, as he himself admits, his counsel is offered "in view of the present distress" (v. 26). Now this does not mean that Paul is offering a "situation ethic" in the modern sense, nor is this a kind of irrelevant "interimsethik". He is simply pointing out that while Christianity is bound to effect sociological and domestic changes, it is not committed to the drastic, harmful disruption of homes and families. Paul recognized that the promiscuity of Corinth presented a challenge to any kind of purity, as well as to domestic felicity.

The followers of Christ therefore must "bend over backwards", as we would say, to defend the honour of the name of Christ in their pagan society. This may mean imposing voluntary and unusual restraints. Christians must abstain even from the appearance of evil (1 Thessalonians 5:22).

Thirdly, while Paul was evidently unmarried at the time of writing 1 Corinthians, he held no brief for celibacy as a higher way of life. Some might have the gift to be celibate, but that was exceptional. For others to try to practise celibacy in the midst of a passionate place like Corinth, or anywhere else for that matter, was like playing with fire. When Paul writes, "it is better to marry than to burn" (i.e. with sexual passions) he is not taking a low view of marriage as if it were a kind of legalized adultery. Rather is he saying that there is nothing wrong with marriage, just as there is nothing wrong with celibacy, providing we undertake them responsibly and wisely. The important thing is to do God's will, and God's will is never likely to lead you into sin. "Only in the Lord" is a general principle of Christian living, as well as a safeguard against an unhappy marriage.

Fourthly, when Paul distinguishes between his own edicts and those of Jesus, he is not suggesting there is a conflict between them. Neither is he saying that his own teaching is an advance on that of his Master. He is merely pointing out that although he has no Dominical word (i.e. saying of Jesus) in answer to this or that specific query, he does have the mind of Christ, through the indwelling Holy Spirit. On this basis he offers his apostolic advice as authentic, divine instruction. It is not second-rate, or of lesser inspiration. Paul's teaching is as authoritative and final in the sense of its inspiration, as is the oral ministry of Jesus. The authority of his teaching did not stem from Paul but from his Master who in calling him to be an apostle gave him that special spiritual acumen necessary for communicating the divine will to the Church.

2. A Variety of Situations

Bearing these things in mind we can now attempt some analysis of Paul's teaching. There appear to be several different cases in view in 1 Corinthians 7.

(a) Firstly, there is the case of married, Christian people who wonder if they should dissolve their marriage and enter into celibacy. Perhaps because of false teaching about sex they have come to regard marriage as second best. Paul writes unequivocally and with Dominical support, that such a divorce would be wrong. What he says is:

> To the married I give this command (not I, but the Lord): A wife must not separate from her husband. But if she does, she must remain unmarried or else be reconciled to her husband, and a husband must not divorce his wife (1 Corinthians 7:10, 11).

There is no question that Paul is talking about divorce in these verses. His word "depart", *chorizō*, according to most reliable Greek lexicons, means divorce in this context.

In the event that the Christian does sue for a divorce on these grounds, Paul teaches that she is not scripturally divorced and should therefore either remain unmarried or be reconciled to her husband. He is not saying that there are no circumstances under which a Christian may be divorced and remarried. He is simply saying up to this point, that a predilection for celibacy is no ground for divorce.

(b) Secondly, Paul deals with the mixed marriage situation where a new convert finds himself married to an unbeliever. The question suggested is whether the new Christian should "up and leave" and divorce his partner. "Certainly not!" would be Paul's answer. If the non-Christian is willing to maintain the marriage then the Christian must not only stay but realize that in staying he has the guarantee of God's help and blessing not only on his non-Christian wife but on their children. To dissolve such a marriage would not only be wrong but would involve forfeiting a beautiful promise.

> But to the rest speak I, not the Lord: If any brother hath a wife that believeth not, and she be pleased to dwell with him, let him not put her away.
>
> And the woman which hath an husband that believeth not, and if he be pleased to dwell with her, let her not leave him.
>
> For the unbelieving husband is sanctified by the wife, and the unbelieving wife is sanctified by the husband: else were your children unclean; but now are they holy (1 Corinthians 7:12–14).

(c) Thirdly, the Apostle deals with the case of the Christian convert who finds himself in a situation where the unbelieving partner decides (probably because of his wife's conversion) to sue for a divorce. What happens in this situation?

Should the Christian put up a fight? Paul's answer is two-fold. On the one hand he says:

The brother or the sister is not under bondage in such cases:

and on the other,

God hath called us to peace (v. 15).

Before discussing Paul's crucial phrase, "not under bondage", we should notice he maintains that even if the unbelieving partner insists on divorce, the Christian should still go on praying for his or her divorced partner. Although the divorce implies the freedom to remarry, the Christian may still decide to remain single in the hope that one day things may be rectified (v. 16). It is surely important to realize in this connection that the act of divorce does not in itself constitute adultery.

There is considerable debate as to the meaning of Paul's phrase: "not under bondage". The English words translate the Greek negative *ou dedoulotai*. The verb *douloō* means quite simply, "to enslave". Paul's point appears to be that if the non-Christian partner chooses to dissolve his marriage and be free to marry again, then the deserted Christian obviously is free as well. She is no longer "enslaved" to the marriage bond which quite apart from her wish or choice, has

40

been broken. The Apostle's use of the perfect tense here suggests not only the immediate but also the continuing freedom of the deserted partner. Without specifically saying it, Paul is apparently implying a freedom to remarry. A further key to his meaning is in Paul's words in v. 27 where he is obviously talking about marriage. He writes:

Art thou bound unto a wife? Seek not to be loosed. Art thou loosed from a wife? Seek not a wife. But and if thou marry, thou hast not sinned (v. 27–28).

Here he contrasts "bound" to a woman, *dedesai gunaiki**, meaning "married", with "loosed", *lusin.* Most lexicons agree that the verb, *luō,* is used metaphorically to describe discharging from debt or divorcing from marriage. The Apostle therefore seems to be saying that if a man has been properly divorced from a woman then for him to remarry is not wrong. He is not recommending remarriage, nor is he encouraging it, he is simply stating a fact. Evidently, under the proper circumstances, the remarriage of a divorced person might be permitted.

* This is the perfect tense of *deō* (*gunaiki*) and by using it Paul is implying that the binding in marriage which took place at some point in the past (perhaps when the party was still a pagan) still is in effect.

3. Explanation of two difficult passages

The first passage is 1 Corinthians 7 verse 39 where Paul writes:

> The wife is bound by the law as long as her husband liveth; but if her husband be dead, she is at liberty to be married to whom she will; only in the Lord.

and the second is Romans 7:1–3:

> Know ye not, brethren, (for I speak to them that know the law) how that the law hath dominion over a man as long as he liveth? For the woman which hath a husband is bound by the law to her husband so long as he liveth; but if the husband be dead, she is loosed from the law of her husband. So then if, while her husband liveth, she is married to another man, she shall be called an adulteress: but if her husband be dead, she is free from that law; so that she is no adulteress, though she be married to another man.

The Greek word for "bound" in both contexts is *dedetai* (as in 1 Corinthians 7:27). Is Paul contradicting himself in these verses by teaching that the marriage bond is indissoluble except by death?

In reply we must say several things. Firstly, Paul would not have taken a position which was in conflict with Christ. We have already observed that he is at pains to cite Christ as his authority wherever possible. Paul knew Jesus taught that divorce was permitted for fornication. Therefore when he speaks of the indissolubility of the marriage bond he is generalizing. If you had questioned him more closely no doubt he would have agreed with Christ's excepting clause. The reason both Christ and Paul speak on occasion without the excepting clause, is because God's ideal is the permanent union of husband and wife. Divorce is always less than the ideal, but as Moses, Paul and his Master all understood only too well, sin has spoiled the ideal and men have hard hearts because of it. Such less-than-ideal situations require legislation, if only to control man's sinful actions and preserve society and family from total disruption and chaos. Secondly, in Romans 7 Paul is not discussing marriage legislation, he is merely using an analogy to illustrate a Christian's relation to the Law. All analogies break down if pressed to prove more than the writer intends.

A final word might be added here in Paul's defence, if indeed that is deemed necessary. We must at least allow Paul consistency. Suppose it were possible to find him guilty of saying one thing to one church in one epistle, and something opposite, to another church in another, that would create problems! Fortunately this is not the case. It is highly unlikely that "in the same breath", just a few sentences apart, Paul would contradict himself on such vital issues as marriage and divorce (1 Corinthians 7:15 and 39). Whatever else Paul may be accused of, he was certainly no "Mr. Facing-both ways"!

It is not Paul who is inconsistent. It is his interpreters. When like the Apostle Peter, they find Paul writing things "hard to understand" (2 Peter 3:26), they try to squeeze him into their own interpretive mould. Fortunately for Paul, he is not that easy to mould.

In summary then, we see that while Paul as Christ's faithful disciple believed in monogamous, permanent marriage, he recognized that fornication or desertion (which was evidently as serious as fornication and as effectively severed the marriage bond) might be grounds for divorce, even for a Christian.

CHAPTER FIVE

Divorce in the Church

Brothers, if someone is caught in a sin, you who are spiritual should restore him gently. But watch yourself, or you may also be tempted. Carry each other's burdens, and in this way you will fulfil the law of Christ (Galatians 6:1–2).

The question is sometimes asked whether people who have been divorced should be welcomed into church fellowship and if so, should they not be excluded from positions of responsibility and service?

Before discussing these questions which are best treated separately – we must make one thing clear. Although the subject of divorce is considered in Scripture, the subject of the reception of divorced people into church membership is not. Therefore, whatever conclusions are drawn and on the basis of whatever criteria, we must be careful to say that they are at best tentative and must be offered in the spirit of Christian love. This is not to say that the church must be careless or permissive in the matter of divorce. Furthermore there may well be scriptural principles of conduct which give a church pause and make it hesitate to "open the floodgates" to people who refuse to accept scriptural direction and authority. However, a church should avoid "speaking as an oracle", particularly where it lacks the specific direction of the oracles of God.

A. Divorce and Church Membership

Let us deal first with the question about receiving into membership in a church, people who have been divorced. There are many factors that must be considered. Of course it goes without saying that no one whether divorced or not, who is not a believer in the Lord Jesus is a member of the Church which is his Body, and should not therefore be a member of a local church. While that may not seem to be immediately relevant to the point of our discussion, it is, because we must always remember that the church is a fellowship of redeemed, forgiven people. We are all sinners saved by grace. Since therefore we are men and women who have experienced forgiveness, who are we to legislate which sins may be forgiven and which not, prior to a person's being welcomed into a church?

Unfortunately, there are many churches that would not hesitate to welcome forgiven thieves, cheats, adulterers, alcoholics, and homicides, but who would exclude divorcees. That does not make too much sense for the followers of the One who

46

was known as "the friend of publicans and sinners". Obviously it implies there are specially stringent criteria applying to the divorced which do not apply even to the once cruel and violent.

Perhaps the argument is that divorce is continuing adultery since once a divorcee is remarried adultery takes place every time there are sexual relations between the partners. This argument is not valid for various reasons. Firstly it regards marriage simply in terms of physical union. That is as unscriptural as it is unrealistic. Once two people are married or remarried, (after divorce) they are bound in a union which is much more than physical and which cannot be dissolved without a further divorce. In any case their former partners may well have entered into other marriages, so that there is no possibility of return and reconciliation. Secondly, the Scriptures which teach that the dissolution of a marriage for other grounds than fornication or desertion is tantamount to committing or causing to commit adultery, do not say that it is in the continuing that the adultery consists. Rather is it in the dissolving and in the remarrying, with all that that implies.

Surely if subsequent to making this mistake and committing this sin, the couple repent of their wrongdoing, they can be forgiven and accepted as bona fide church members. Of course there will always be the question of whether the repentance is genuine, but fortunately forgiveness, in that sense, is a divine prerogative. Our Lord's criterion was, "by their fruits you will know them". If we arbitrarily excommunicate the divorced are we not causing unnecessary grief to many innocent people? Of course it can be argued academically that both partners are guilty and that it takes two to pick a quarrel. It is certainly true in life that both parties in a divorce suit are involved in the sense that both have made mistakes. However, anyone who has tried to help counsel in divorce situations, will tell you that there is, more often than not, a guilty party and an innocent party. Indeed if we lack practical precedent, the Bible itself recognized that there might be an "innocent victim" and in such case there was special legislation (Deuteronomy 22:24).

Although we have by inference referred to conversions after divorce we must deal with this matter quite specifically. For example, if people who have been divorced come later to trust Christ as Saviour, are they too to be excluded from the church? Does conversion take care of the problem of divorce in the sense that regeneration means a new beginning? Paul's words to the Corinthians, "Therefore, if anyone is in Christ, he is a new creation; the old has gone, the new has come" (2 Corinthians 5:17), are sometimes quoted in support of this position.

It certainly seems strange logic which tells a newly converted, divorced couple who have never

48

read their Bibles or had any idea of what Christianity is all about, that there is no room for them in the church. Of course we may argue that marriage is a human institution rather than a Christian institution and because of that conversion to Christ is irrelevant. However, surely the principle of "by the law is the knowledge of sin" applies here. If somebody has lived in total ignorance of the Bible and its ethical requirements for the married, we cannot regard the divorce of that person in the same light as the divorce of someone who has "sinned against the light". This is not to cancel the validity of the non-Christian marriage bond but simply to act responsibly in the face of actual, life situations, in our contemporary society.

Paul evidently accepted pagan marriage contracts and urged his readers not to breach them by filing for divorce. At the same time he refused to lock Christians into an impossible situation by saying that if the pagan partner initiated the divorce the Christian must refuse to accept it and remain unmarried. The Apostle was realistic enough to accept non-Christian marriage, and for that matter non-Christian divorce. What he refused to accept was "any and every cause" as sufficient ground for divorce. This is why he insisted on "being reconciled or remaining unmarried", for a Christian who initiated divorce proceedings for other than the scriptural grounds of fornication. Since Paul did not state in

1 Corinthians 7 that divorce before conversion precluded church membership it seems obvious that he did not hold this view. He quite clearly excommunicates Christians who despite their profession of faith in Christ, persist in immoral or idolatrous habits (1 Corinthians 5:9–13). What people do who have no knowledge of the lordship of Christ is one thing. How Christians behave is another! The standard for the believer is much higher. We must be doubly on guard. At the same time we must not forget the "pit whence we were digged" nor refuse to stretch out the hand of Christian welcome to those who are even now struggling out of theirs.

One other situation comes to mind. Suppose two Christian people, a husband and wife, who have both been divorced (on non-biblical grounds) from other Christian spouses, come to seek church membership what should our attitude be to them? Obviously the offences committed by these two Christian divorcees are more serious. They are regenerate and they had opportunity to read and understand Scripture yet they still went against the scriptural teaching about marriage and divorce. There may well be a number of mitigating circumstances in this situation. We do not know for example, whether these people were "alive" Christians at the time of their divorce. Were they attending church? Were they backsliding? Were they aware of the teaching of scripture about marriage? These and many other questions come to mind. Whatever the circumstances, the chances are they were both out of fellowship with the Lord when they sued for their divorce. This would certainly be the case if they both obtained their divorces because of and in order to marry each other. In that case not only was their action wrong but their motivation was wrong.

However, at this point, what is the church to say? It is, of course, impossible to legislate. All we can suggest is that the church should make it very plain to the couple, that their past actions cannot be condoned and they must be shown from scripture why the church feels that way. It might also be appropriate to ask the couple to admit that what they did was wrong and give some indication of genuine repentance during a suitable probationary period. Once this is done, unless we want to take the position that there is no forgiveness for such a couple, it would probably be in the spirit of Christ to receive them. What they did may have been wrong but it is done and cannot be undone, without further, messy divorce proceedings. Therefore we accept their *de facto* relationship and try to help them go forward to new places of blessing in Christ. Let us remember that whatever the unpardonable sin may be, it is not divorce and remarriage!

B. Divorce and Christian Leadership

We come to the second question, as to whether divorced people once restored, should be given positions of leadership and responsibility in the church. Again this is a difficult question and involves many secondary issues. Perhaps it will help set our perspective right if we remind ourselves that divorce and remarriage aside, not all Christians are eligible for positions of leadership. There are all kinds of criteria for leadership in a local church. Many of these are spelled out by Paul when he discusses the subject of elders and deacons, in his Pastoral Epistles.

First and foremost any Christian responsibility or service must reflect our divinely given charisma or spiritual gift. Even the leadership of the Church is to be the province of those who are "gifted to rule", and whom the Holy Spirit has endowed for the task (Romans 12:8, Acts 20:28, 1 Corinthians 12:28). It is not enough for a person to be attractive, persuasive, experienced, clever or wealthy, to hold office in the church. Divine election must take precedence over human selection.

In addition to this divine endowment for responsibility there are stringent social, moral, personal and marital requirements. In other words not all gifted leaders should be allowed to lead. They must see to it that their lives give no cause for shame or question, as far as the corporate witness of the church is concerned. How a man behaves in his home, how he treats his wife, how he rears his children, are all accepted criteria for Christian service. It is not enough that a man be righteous but that he be seen to be righteous, both in his home and outside it, if he is to qualify for leadership.

Bearing those high standards in mind we can better examine the question of the eligibility of a divorced person for a place of responsibility or leadership in the Christian church. If a strict monogamy was imposed on the leaders of the New Testament church can we suggest anything less today? Of course it may be argued that Paul's words to Timothy and Titus (1 Timothy 3:2, Titus 1:6) are directed against a polygamous man rather than against one who has divorced and remarried. That may be true to some degree, although scholars are generally agreed that polygamy was not a problem in Paul's contemporary society and would therefore not be in his thought. However, since Paul allows widowed people to remarry (Romans 7:1–3), it might well be argued that he is explicitly precluding the divorced and remarried from Christian office. Commenting on 1 Timothy 3:2 and Titus 1:6, F. F. Bruce writes:

> More probably these passages have in view persons who have been divorced and then remarried (the same applies of 1 Timothy 5:9). Legalised polygamy

was so rare in the Jewish and Graeco-Roman world after the first century AD that we can scarcely think that the apostle is primarily forbidding a man to be an elder if he has more than one wife at a time.*

This may seem like a strange suggestion in our permissive society. However, our norms must be not what is socially acceptable, but what is scripturally required. Some of us can remember times not too far distant, when a divorced man would have found his divorce an impediment in his pursuit even for public office let alone an office in the church. However varying society's standards the authority of scripture remains unchanging. It will serve no useful purpose to attempt to accommodate scripture to modern, social pressures.

Someone will complain that to debar divorced Christians from leadership or responsibility in the church is to treat them as second class citizens or to introduce a double standard. Surely, they imply we must forgive and forget! If we are willing to include them as church members then why exclude them from service? After all, church history has its Paul, its Augustine, its Luther and its Müller to mention only a few of the great, changed leaders who have made their mark for God. Certainly no one would claim that in their pre-Christian days these men were paragons of

* F. F. Bruce, *Answers to Questions* p.115.

moral virtue. If God could use such men then why disqualify divorcees from church office?

These certainly sound like reasonable arguments but as we have already noted, responsibility or leadership in a church requires high moral and spiritual qualifications. The reason is no doubt that when an ordinary member does something questionable then that is personal, although having an effect on the whole church. When a leader's conduct is in question it is viewed as more serious and representative because of his special office. A Christian leader will be viewed by his non-Christian neighbours as acting or speaking "ex cathedra". In other words the testimony and reputation of the Church will be at stake.

There is Old Testament support for the idea of a high conjugal standard being required of spiritual leaders. In Leviticus 21 the ceremonial requirements for the priests are set out. Among them we read,

> They shall not take a woman that is a harlot, or profane; neither shall they take a woman put away from her husband; for he is holy unto his God (v.7).

Clearly divorce would disqualify a man from holding spiritual office in Israel. It is unlikely that the Christian church shuld accept a lower standard.

The fact that divorced person is excluded from

55

leadership in the church obviously does not mean that he cannot engage in Christian service. There are many areas of need and work requiring our attention, and whether we are single, married, divorced or divorced and remarried is not the point. It is whether we are willing to put our hand to the plough and our necks to the work of the Lord. The church will always have need of "back room boys" and the competition is nothing like as fierce in the back room!

CHAPTER SIX

Questions and Answers

Listen now to me and I will give you some advice, and may God be with you
(Exodus 18:19).

There are so many difficult questions that can be asked about the subject of divorce that we cannot possibly deal with all of them. We shall attempt to focus on a few and hope that the conclusions drawn may be helpful both to those who experience the pain of divorce and to those who offer counsel and become involved in helping people. It goes without saying that we shall not resolve all the academic issues that might be raised. In any case our purpose is to be practical not theoretical. We have already looked briefly at scriptural teaching about divorce and tried to understand some basic principles. When we offer suggestions which are not based on the actual words of Scripture we do so humbly and conscious of our liability to err. Some might advise against even attempting to offer such suggestions. However, we cannot agree, and sense an ever-deepening need to meet and help people where we find them. Shepherds are asked, not to give sheep road maps but to walk with them through shadowed valleys. Sometimes men and women are in such entanglement and difficulty that they are even beyond situations contemplated in Scripture. This does not mean that we cannot help them. Too many Christians think of their church as a club for the socially acceptable, rather than as a spiritual hospital for the mending of lives and families.

Question 1

If a Christian woman knows that her husband wants a divorce but he has no grounds on which to sue for one, is it ever right for her to initiate the divorce?

Answer

There are many fine Christian women who have put up with a promiscuous and disagreeable husband for many years and have felt that they cannot give in to this husband's repeated requests for a divorce. Obviously one can only marvel at their Christian patience. However, we must ask whether there is not a scriptural alternative open to such women. Does a Christian wife's commitment to Scripture preclude her granting a divorce?

58

It would seem that the "Pauline privilege" of 1 Corinthians 7 covers this situation although it is not specifically in Paul's view. He teaches that if a Christian woman (probably in his mind, a convert from paganism) discovers that her husband insists on divorce, then she may acquiesce and allow him to go, without being guilty of disobeying the Lord. Paul's dictum is that "the believer is not bound" or "enslaved". On the basis of this statement we are probably not wrong in thinking that Paul would have approved the Christian's initiating the divorce proceedings if that was the only way the non-Christian could get his often repeated wish.

Question 2

What about the marriage of a Christian woman to a divorced man who has become a Christian since his divorce from his former wife? The grounds of his divorce were neither of those contemplated in the New Testament. His former wife has remarried.

Answer

This question has a number of ramifications. First of all, since his former wife has remarried there is no possibility of reconciliation. Secondly, since the man's divorce has been finalized, he is legally free to remarry. The fact that he has become a Christian means that the new marriage will be between two Christians which is the minimum requirement for any Christian wedding. The most serious consideration here is whether the Christian woman by marrying this divorced man will involve herself in an adulterous union.

The fact is that the teachings of Jesus and Paul are both directed to believers, and it is questionable whether we can impose Christian ethics on non-Christian people. We have already seen that our Lord's standards are impossible for an unregenerate person to attain. The whole thrust of his ethic is that until the tree is changed the fruit remains the same. Christianity is not the imposing of an external standard of ethics, no matter how wonderful it may be. It is the remaking of the man himself so that he, regenerated and indwelt by the Holy Spirit, can live in conformity with the will of God.

Both our Lord and Paul were idealists in the sense that they based their teaching regarding marriage, on the divine ideal as evident in creation. God's plan, they insisted, was that a man and his wife should be united so closely and permanently in marriage that the two became one flesh. However, while committed to this ideal, both were realistic enough to recognize that sin has ruined it. Men and woman as well as their relationships are spoiled by sin. This condition is irremediable apart from divine grace.

It would seem that neither Jesus' nor Paul's teaching about marriage and divorce is directed to non-Christians. Even the Mosaic legislation which was an attempt to ameliorate a deteriorating, social situation in Israel recognized the hopeless sinfulness of man. Evidently men were treating their wives shamefully and abandoning them to a life of misery. By requiring the writing of a bill of divorcement Moses' law at least established the fact that the wife who was put away was no longer under her former husband's jurisdiction but was legally free to marry again, and hopefully, discover happiness.

As we have already seen, there is considerable discussion as to the grounds for divorce under the Mosaic legislation as interpreted by the Rabbis. There seemed to be considerable flexibility and the technical term "uncleanness" (Deuteronomy 24:1) was used to cover almost every contingency, from whether a wife proved to be a shrew to whether she burnt her husband's dinner.

Why discuss all these details again here? Just to make it clear that whatever may be the grounds for divorce that are allowed by this or that passage of Scripture, they apply to those who know the Lord of Scripture. We cannot impose them on unbelievers. We may hope that secular jurisprudence will take account of Scripture but we certainly have no guarantee of this.

Paul evidently recognized divorce as prescribed by a secular (that is pagan) society, for non-Christians. If a Christian happened to be the innocent party in such an action then this did not in Paul's view, invalidate the divorce, nor require the divorced Christian to remain unmarried.

Bearing these factors in mind it would seem to be a fair deduction from the total inference of Scripture that a Christian woman is free to marry a divorced man who has become a Christian even though the grounds of his divorce were not such as might be permitted for a Christian. She will not thereby incur the sentence of becoming an adulteress.

Question 3

What about a Christian spouse who is divorced by her husband who himself professed to be a Christian yet sued for divorce on other than "Christian grounds"? Is she free to remarry, since her former husband has remarried?

Answer

Here again we have a case which is not uncommon, yet which is not contemplated in Scripture. We must therefore again try to apply general, scriptural principles and offer practical help.

Although the former husband professed faith in Christ it would appear that he did not act as a Christian nor in accord with Scripture. Because of his disobedience of Scripture the husband deliberately put himself outside the divine directive. He acted in fact as a non-Christian would act. It would therefore appear that he is in the same category as the unbelieving husband of 1 Corinthians 7 who divorced his wife but in so doing left her free to remarry. To refuse this point of view is to make the innocent party suffer for the guilty party's sin. Both Jesus and Paul, aware of the divine ideal as they were, met people where they were and in their particular situations of need. The Church today can do no less. Our task is not legalistically to place unwieldy burdens on people's shoulders, but to offer sympathetic and concerned Christian help.

Question 4

Is it ever right for a Christian to initiate a legal separation?

Answer

The idea of legal separation is not contemplated in Scripture. Divorce, in Scripture, as in Jewish thought, was dissolution of marriage, not simply the physical separation of husband and wife. The nearest we come to this idea in the Bible is where Paul offers counsel to the married, Christian spouse of an incorrigible, non-Christian husband. There he seems to say that if the Christian finds it impossible to live with the non-Christian, (and only if,) she may divorce him (*chorizō*) but she is not free to remarry (1 Corinthians 7:11). Although the wife has initiated the divorce, perhaps for her own physical safety or that of her children, she has done no wrong. She would be wrong if she remarried however, because that would cancel any opportunity of reconciliation. Suppose the husband, subsequent to the divorce, marries someone else, then presumably the divorced wife would be free to remarry. That this is Paul's meaning seems evident from his phrase "but if she depart (*chorizō* means "divorce") let her remain unmarried". Obviously the woman would not be able to "remain unmarried", if "depart" simply meant separation. She is still married, as long as she is only separated, but not divorced from her husband.

A legal separation may well be a saving solution for a Christian wife who for one or many reasons finds it impossible to continue living with her husband, and yet wishes to leave open the possibility of reconciliation. Under the provisions of a present-day legal separation, she has the protection and provision of the law and yet she has not initiated a divorce proceeding which she may feel would in her case, be contrary to Scripture.

Question 5

Is the New Testament teaching about divorce

applicable to Christians only or to people in general?

Answer

This is a more difficult question than it appears on the surface and we need to think carefully about issues involved. There is little doubt that while the teaching of Jesus and Paul applies primarily to believers it would seem to have a wider application. To doubt this is rather like saying that the teaching of Scripture applies only to Christians which is manifestly absurd. In fact it is the "entrance of God's word that gives light" to non-Christians too.

The answer to this question lies not in the "either or" approach, but in "both and". In other words, the teaching of Scripture is applicable primarily to Christians but also to non-Christians. While Christian living obviously implies Christian life, God's requirements and standards are valid for all his creatures. There is divine revelation through nature, through conscience, through Scripture and through Christ. Furthermore this revelation is as consistent as it is available. The enjoyment of the benefits of these media of revelation is of course contingent upon their being accepted. Whether a person has arrived at the place of total commitment to Christ as Lord or not, he may still enjoy blessing through submission to Scripture. Ultimately of course, such submission will lead to surrender to Christ because the purpose of Scripture is to testify about and bring us to Christ (John 5:39–40).

Having considered these general principles let us come back to the applicability to non-Christian people of biblical principles concerning marriage and divorce. It is significant that when Jesus deals with the question of divorce he directs his questioners back to the Creation narrative. In other words he views marriage not as a Christian institution but as a divine institution for man as his creature. Marriage has to do with men and women as they are, not simply as they are regenerate in Christ. This is surely most significant and has a direct bearing on the question under consideration.

It would seem reasonable therefore to say that whenever we find people who are willing to accept the mandate of Scripture we find happy marriages and homes. The Bible is God's word to man as man and applies to him in all his relationships. However, where husbands and wives try to fashion their relationship on Scripture but refuse to submit to the Lord of Scripture, they will create a disastrous dichotomy.

Surely it was this that our Lord's first disciples realized when they heard his reply about marriage and divorce. They saw immediately that his standard was impossible of attainment without the saving grace of God in the heart.

In summary then we may say that biblical

teaching about marriage and divorce is always in man's best interests. Whenever we accept Jesus' teaching we benefit from it. We do ourselves and our families a great disservice when we opt to "go it alone", counter to Scripture, Jesus' teaching applies to all mankind but it is practically realizable only for those who submit to his Lordship. The issue is not academic, it is spiritual. He himself said: "If any man is willing to do God's will he shall know" (John 7:17).

Having said this, as Christians, we must be careful that we do not coldly legislate for non-Christians on the basis of Scripture. It is one thing for us to bow to Christ's authoritative word, it is another thing to lay it down as law for people who as yet do not know our Master. We shall be wise to remember that "if any man be in Christ [and only if!] he is a new creation" (2 Corinthians 5:17).

Question 6

If my church's position on divorce is different from other Christian opinions I have read, what attitude should I adopt as a divorcee?

Answer

Again, there are many side issues involved in this question and without knowing what kind of a church is in view, it is difficult to be specific.

However, generally speaking, if your church is an evangelical, Bible-believing church where Christ is honoured, you will be wise to be extremely careful about taking a contrary stand on divorce. After all godly men differ on some of these issues but seek to offer obedience to Christ.

It would be wise to discuss your understanding of the matter of divorce with your leaders and to ask them for a clarification of their views and the Scriptures upon which they base them. If it is evident that the Church's position is scripturally supportable then you will be wise to cooperate. Consider another church home only after you have carefully exhausted all other possibilities and have honestly decided that the point of view advocated by your present church is quite untenable in the light of Scripture. At all cost avoid returning home to your Church after attending some cosy little conference on "Divorce and the Family", intent on putting your elders right even at the expense of causing division in the church.

Question 7

Is it ever right for a Christian to initiate a divorce proceeding?

Answer

On the basis of Scripture we may say that in one situation it might not be wrong for a Christian to sue for a divorce. However before we look at this situation let us immediately say that it is not always necessary for a Christian to seek a divorce even though he may have scriptural grounds for so doing.

The only scriptural ground on which a Christian may initiate a divorce is "for fornication". We have discussed suggested interpretations of this term elsewhere. We conclude that it means illicit, extra-marital sex which is engaged in quite deliberately and persistently. While a Christian might argue that a single act of adultery on the part of his spouse constitutes scriptural ground for divorce, this might well contravene the real meaning of Scripture. Surely Jesus' excepting clause must not be used as a weapon against a spouse who falls, in a moment of temptation. If it is used in this way then one wonders which party is more blameworthy. After all, Jesus said that the lustful look is tantamount to committing adultery (Matthew 5:28). Whoever would survive if there were legislation against such attitudes? The reason for Jesus' excepting clause is not to provide an excuse for divorce, but to guard against divorce except under the most extreme necessity.

In case someone objects that there is another ground on which a Christian may initiate divorce proceedings, namely desertion, we should note the following. While desertion may be a permissable ground of divorce on the basis of Paul's teaching in 1 Corinthians 7, he clearly does not envisage a Christian initiating such a proceeding. The Christian may acquiesce and accept the fact of divorce for desertion, with its consequent freedom to remarry, but he will not make the first move. The principle is clear:

> If any brother hath a wife that believeth not and she is pleased to dwell with him, let him not put her away. And the woman which hath a husband that believeth not and he is pleased to dwell with her, let her not leave (*aphietō*) him (1 Corinthians 7:13).

Christianity as Paul understood it, tended to improve and bring blessing into human relationships, rather than destroy them. Clearly, in the case the Apostle is reviewing, the marriage contract had been entered into prior to either partner's becoming a Christian. The conversion of either the husband or wife in no way invalidated the marriage. It was considered to be the same binding covenant as if two Christians were married. By the same token the divorce proceedings if initiated by the non-Christian partner and presumably before some pagan court, were accepted as valid by the Apostle. In other words while marriage and divorce before pagan authorities were contemplated and recognized by the New Testament, pagan grounds for divorce were not. If we keep this in mind we shall see that there is no contradiction between the teaching of Christ and the teaching of Paul, as some suggest. Paul did not invent a second ground for divorce. He concurred fully with Jesus' teaching namely, that ideally marriage was indissoluble. However, where sin patently marred the ideal and fornication was persisted in, the partner who was sinned against might initiate proceedings for divorce. When Paul faces a situation not contemplated in our Lord's teaching (i.e. a "mixed marriage"), he still insists on Christ's 'excepting clause' but envisages the possibility of a divorce being initiated by the non-Christian partner. This, he says, would free the Christian from all obligation to the marriage. We must understand that the so-called "Pauline privilege" does not grant the Christian the privilege of initiating a divorce on any other ground than that permitted by Jesus. To say that it does is not only to create confusion but to suggest a conflict between Jesus and Paul whose words were inspired in each case by the same Holy Spirit.

Question 8

When a couple wish to remarry after being involved in divorce, should a minister agree to solemnize such a marriage in the usual way or should certain conditions be suggested for this occasion?

Answer

If the minister is satisfied that he can in all good
faith be involved in the marriage of this couple
then he might want to make a few suggestions
about the actual wedding service. For example,
he might be wise to recommend a quiet, more
private ceremony. After all, the first marriage
which was probably performed amidst all the
quasi-pageantry and extravagant ostentation of
contemporary nuptials proved little more than a
charade. So, why repeat the performance? On
that initial occasion, presuming it was a church
wedding, solemn oaths were uttered and
promises made, not only in the presence of the
congregation but before God. Can this all be so
lightly brushed aside and forgotten? Did the
words "for better, for worse" mean nothing? Is
there not the least regret that having begun
under such ideal circumstances the marriage
soon deteriorated into confusion and failure?
Such questions surely point in the direction of
modesty and Christian decorum.

Not only should the occasion be decorous but
the very words of the marriage ceremony should
include some reference to previous failure. It
would augur well for this new beginning if the
couple gave some public expression to their regret
and repentance for having failed to live up to the
vows they made on a previous occasion. Such
sincere and well considered words might have a

chastening and salutary effect not only on the couple themselves but also on their immediate family and friends who have no doubt experienced some measure of pain through the divorce. Furthermore it will make it obvious that while the church wishes to act in forgiving and generous love, it must not sweep under the rug anything and everything which may be spiritually embarrassing. After all the church has a solemn responsibility in representing her Master, to help her younger members understand the seriousness of life and the solemnity of marriage. Even if under certain special and unusual circumstances the church agrees to remarriage after divorce, she must take her stand unequivocally and courageously for the sanctity and permanence of Christian marriage. In so doing the church is not being piously obscurantist as her critics aver. She is simply trying to represent her holy Lord who although loving sinners and sacrificing himself to save them, is unalterably fixed in his hatred of sin and deceit. The following excerpt from a recent wedding service suggests what we have in mind.

Marriage is to be entered into reverently, discreetly, advisedly, soberly and in the fear of God, duly considering the causes for which it was ordained. These are: companionship, comfort and happy family life.

Into this holy estate 'X' and 'Y' come now to be joined.

They humbly acknowledge before God past failure and broken vows and having experienced the saving grace of God, commit themselves to Christian marriage. If anyone knows of any just cause why they may not be so joined, let him now speak or hereafter remain silent.

Question 9

If a Christian senses that his marriage is over to all intent and purpose, and that he is living in a state of "spiritual divorce" is it not better to terminate the marriage legally by a divorce, than to maintain a pretence?

Answer

Once again, this question has many facets and needs to be stripped of several false assumptions and emptional overtones. First of all we might ask, what is "spiritual divorce"? It is certainly a concept foreign to Scripture except in the metaphorical language used to describe Jehovah's broken relationship with Israel and Judah (cf. Isaiah 50:1 and Jeremiah 3:8). However it is clear that the questioner has something other than this in mind.

The thinking behind the term "spiritual divorce" is that marriage is essentially an idealized, spiritual, relationship. It suggests that if a couple find they have "fallen in love" and they decide to perpetuate a deep relationship, call it

74

"going steady" if you like, then they may consider themselves "spiritually married". Consequently anything is permissible. On this basis, legalization of the marriage before a judge or getting married before a minister in church become redundant and unnecessary. However ethereal and liberated this view of marriage seems to be, it is much more closely related to a debased "situation ethic" than to the ethics of the Bible.

Granted, the best marriages are conceived in heaven and consummated on earth, but Christians will be wise to go through a marriage ceremony and accept the binding, legal contract of marriage. It is not hard to imagine the dangers and potential promiscuity masked behind this concept of "spiritual marriage". It is a case of easy come, easy go.

There are many reasons why a Christian will want to go through a proper, legal procedure of marriage. Firstly, as Christians we are called to recognize and submit to the authority of the state (unless of course it attempts to usurp the place of God – Acts 5:29). Secondly, a properly contracted marriage is essential for the protection of offspring. Quite apart from the stigma of illegitimacy for which no child will ever thank its parents, there are the practical necessities of the law in relation to property ownership and the like. Even in our permissive, contemporary western society which has accepted trial marriage, common law marriage, homosexual marriage and other strange arrangements, it is still necessary to secure legal documents for the sake of all concerned. All this points to the fickleness, not to mention the selfish sinfulness, of the human heart, which is all too ready to love things and use people for its own ends. Thirdly, without prescribing a certain kind of religious ceremony, the Bible everywhere recognizes such an event and Jesus graced such a ceremony by his presence and first miracle in Cana of Galilee, as the Prayer Book notes. Obviously the "till-death-do-us-part", exclusive covenant-contract between two consenting adult persons is the heart of marriage but this is best publicly proclaimed and ratified, especially in our morally ambiguous society.

If "spiritual marriage" is so hazardous and unbiblical, how much more so "spiritual divorce"! It is unthinkable that a Christian could condone such a pathetically secular attitude towards marriage. Presumably he entered marriage not only with his partner but with God. Dare he now say, "Well, the marriage is over between us (i.e. "spiritually"), so let's get it over legally"?

Surely the Christian approach must be different from that! Let us not advocate the externalizing and actualization of a divorce which we claim is already an accomplished fact spiritually. Let us rather pray, plead and work together for the removal and cleansing away of wrong heart attitudes. If the grace of God is anything it can accomplish the miracle of restoring broken relationships between Christians. It will take time, effort, patience and more than these, but it will certainly be worth it! Marriages can be made to work. We can learn to love. Forget about the romanticized, Hollywood version of love and get back to the New Testament, where love is not only commanded but given. We also do well to remember that in Bible times, as in many contemporary cultures, marriages are arranged by parents. Surprising though it may seem to us Westerners, such marriages can still work; can still provide happiness; and, if statistics mean anything, are less vulnerable to divorce.

Finally, there is the case of the questioner who is genuinely concerned about pretending that his marriage is more secure than it really is, on the basis that pretence is lying. The answer is two-fold. Firstly, even if our marriage is not all that we hope other people think it is, it is still worth preserving as something which we contracted before God. Secondly, we need to seek a better sense of values. The cultivating of harmony and love in marriage is infinitely more important than the perpetuation of a "99.99% whiter than white" honesty attitude. No marriage relationship is perfect but a Christian marriage "warts and all" is a million times better than the enslavement of "free love".

Question 10

When a Christian spouse is deserted or divorced by his or her partner will this inevitably damage the children of the marriage? Would it not be better to insist on keeping the marriage together for the family's sake?

Answer

These are difficult questions and obviously people who have experienced the trauma of a broken marriage may well have diferent opinions. Before attempting to offer advice let us consider some scriptural principles. Firstly, Paul clearly teaches that where a Christian seeks to honour God and obey him, particularly in the matter of marriage and family life, God grants special grace. For example, if a Christian finds herself married to a non-Christian and seeks to do all she can to preserve that marriage, her children become God's special concern (1 Corinthians 7:14). If, on the other hand, she acts hastily and dissolves her marriage on the basis that her husband is not a believer and may therefore have an unhelpful effect on the children, then she forfeits that special divine benediction.

Secondly, and this is specially true where the children are themselves Christians, God is concerned about families and will grant sufficient grace to cope with even the extreme sadness and difficulty caused by marital breakdown

(2 Corinthians 12:9). In fact it sometimes seems to be true that children who have gone through the experience of a break-up have grown stronger through adversity. There is a principle that testing in the crucible of affliction purifies the metal of our faith. It is sometimes said that "broken homes produce broken homes". However, this is not necessarily so if the home is a Christian home, especially where through no real fault of her own a woman finds herself and her children abandoned. Some of the greatest Christian characters have been moulded for blessing through the tragedy of a broken home. Compensatory relationships have been developed and roots have been strengthened through the buffeting winds of adversity.

Thirdly, we must remember that God has promised to be a husband to the widow and a father to the fatherless. These are not empty words, but divine promises that can be counted on. The church has a special responsibility to families in crisis. In fact, one criterion of the authenticity of our Christianity is whether we are willing to become involved with people who have experienced broken relationships (James 1:27).

In passing we should observe that while divorce and separation are always sad and liable to have a harmful effect on families, lasting scars are not inevitable. Sometimes in an effort to hold the family together at all cost, we can inflict

79

more damage on our children than by allowing divorce to happen. Children are extraordinarily resilient psychologically and spiritually. What they need most is the security of knowing they are loved and wanted. Where parents divorce, they should be at pains to explain things to their children. For example they should tell them that while mother and father are severing their relationship, they are doing so without attributing blame to the family. Children should not be used as pawns in marital chess games but treated with dignity and respect. They should be assured that the relationship between them and both their parents will be maintained on the same natural and affectionate terms as always. The divorce while obviously a family affair is essentially between two people, and the parties to it should recognize that and not try to blame or punish others for it, least of all their children.

Question 11

Although it may be argued that the divorced are disqualified from leadership in the church, is there not an exception to be made in the case of the person whose divorce pre-dated his conversion to Christ?

Answer

This question certainly raises a vital issue, and

draws an important distinction. First, there can be no question that God's grace is the all sufficient remedy for sin. Once a man is forgiven, he is forgiven. If subsequent to his conversion a man's personal life has been exemplary, his domestic life above reproach, and his spiritual gifts for leadership evident, and he has matured spiritually, there would seem to be no reason to preclude him from office. However, we shall be wise to exercise caution.

Certainly his situation is different from that of a man who as an informed believer, perhaps even as a recognized Christian leader, deliberately enters a divorce proceeding. In this latter case we have someone who is apparently and perhaps arrogantly "sinning against the light". Obviously such a man should be denied positions of responsibility and leadership.

In his instructions regarding Christian leaders, Paul is at pains to stress the importance of right attitudes. It is possible that an individual may have all the proper conjugal, domestic and social qualifications and yet have anything but a genuinely gracious Christian spirit. Such a man, be he single or "once-married", is less likely to make a true shepherd than one who has erred and strayed like a lost sheep but has then returned to the Shepherd and Guardian of his soul (1 Peter 2:25). In point of fact, and this is the heart of the matter, the New Testament is far more concerned about the exercise of gift in service than it is about elevation to office in the church. Generally speaking biblical ecclesiology knows nothing of appointment to office. It is simply concerned about the due recognition of those who are gifted to rule by the Holy Spirit.

Question 12

Since the family is in peril and divorce is so prevalent, can you suggest some basic guidelines or even guarantees for happy Christian marriage?

Answer

To answer this question adequately would require another book. However, since the matter is urgent and certainly related to our subject we will try to offer some "capsule advice".

For a strong and happy marriage: (1) follow the Maker's instructions; (2) cultivate proper attitudes; and (3) avoid recognized hazards.

We shall now examine these recommendations more closely.

1. Follow the Maker's instructions.

The last thing most people do when they purchase an expensive new appliance is, read the manufacturers instructions! Little wonder they are soon faced with costly repair bills or worse, forced to discard the appliance. This is exactly like many people's attitude to marriage.

They rush into this most beautiful, yet delicate of all life's relationships without consulting God our Maker's manual – the Bible.

The Bible is full of helpful instructions about marriage and the home. Interestingly enough while the ratio of divorce to marriage in secular North American society has climbed to almost one in two; in Christian groups where the authority of Scripture is still recognized the ratio is about one in forty. That has to say something!

The following scriptures are explicit and offer a wealth of instruction.

Deuteronomy 6:4–9	1 Timothy 2:8–15
1 Corinthians 7 and 11:3	Titus 2:1–8
Ephesians 5:22–6:4	1 Peter 3:1–7

Bearing these and other related references in mind, we discover the Bible teaches that married people will be wise to:

(A) Make Christ the Lord and senior partner in their marriage, accepting his Word as their guide.

(B) Recognize the sanctity, permanence, unity, mutuality and divine purpose of marriage.

(C) Submit to God's "chain of command" in the home.

(D) Accept their God-given marital responsibilities. These responsibilities at a minimum are:

(i) *for the husband*
To love sacrificially, like Christ,
To provide and care for his wife (and family),
To rule his home under Christ, without domineering.

(ii) *for the wife*
To support, honour and respect her husband,
To endeavour to be a contented and practical homemaker.

Then, when the dual relationship of marriage broadens into the multiple relationship of family, the Bible offers further direction. It teaches that parents are:

(A) To love and nurture their children;
(B) To teach them by example as well as precept;
(C) To discipline but not exasperate them;
(D) To provide for but not spoil them.

By the same token Scripture commands children to offer obedience, honour and respect to their parents. Then, just as parents are to provide for their children when they are small, so those children are to return this grace and provide for their parents when they grow old and have needs.

2. Cultivate proper attitudes.
A marriage, or for that matter a family, will be

enriched if each partner deliberately cultivates proper attitudes towards the other(s). Here are a few suggestions:

(A) See to it that we love one another with the kind of love that gives rather then demands.

(B) Practise the art of taking time to share together in work, in play, in prayer and in worship.

(C) Respect each person in our family as an intrinsically valuable individual, and reject the urge to squeeze everyone into our approved pattern.

(D) Talk, never sulk! Remember the two magic phrases that cement relationships are, "I love you!" and, "I'm sorry!"

(E) Cultivate gratitude for little things and never hesitate to say, "Thank you".

(F) Be patient with others, remembering that you may not always be completely right.

For some biblical perspectives on attitudes, read 1 Corinthians 13 or Galatians 5:22–23. Paul knew a good deal about human nature.

3. Avoid recognized hazards.

If we are aware of the hazardous shoals and rocks that shipwreck most marriages and precipitate divorce, it will help us navigate a safe passage. Let's talk about some of the more notorious hazards.

(A) A lack of fiscal policy and a failure to understand that "the love of money is a root of all kinds of evil" causes many divorces.

(B) Parents and friends represent one of life's greatest treasures but neither must be allowed to come between husband and wife. Two important lessons in marriage are learning to "leave" and learning to "cleave".

(C) Sex is a very beautiful and essential part of marriage, but misunderstood, or used to manipulate a spouse, it can be devastating.

(D) Children are a blessing from God but if parents do not stand together both for their children and against them some times, there will never be harmony in marriage nor in the home. Parents do well to remember that, generally speaking, their relationship with each other must take precedence over their relationships with their children!

(E) Religious convictions, unless discussed, understood and agreed upon by both parties to a marriage, will cause discord or even disruption.

There are many more practical questions that might be considered, but clearly space is limited. We submit in conclusion that complex and tragic though some situations have become, it is only we ourselves who put ourselves beyond God's help. He is always there. However much God hates our sins, and let's face it, he hates divorce (Malachi 2:16), God still loves sinners! So often the problem is our unwillingness to acknow ledge our sin, confess it to the Lord and then believe that we are forgiven (1 John 1:9). Remember, this is absolutely true, no matter what other people may say, even though they be well-meaning Christians!

In case you are wondering about seeking help, remember that it is not a sign of spiritual strength to try to bear your burden alone. A burden shared is a burden lifted. Do not hesitate to seek the wise counsel of an experienced Christian counsellor. Let Christ the burden-bearer carry your load through the agency of one of his trained and willing servants.

To any who read these pages but who do not yet enjoy an intimate living relationship with God through faith in Jesus Christ – remember the Chinese proverb: "The longest journey begins with the first step." Let that step be the step of trusting in the Saviour who loved you enough to die for you and who lives to share as deeply as you will let him in all your sorrows as well as in all your joys.

87

Finally, here is a prayer for those in crisis.

Grant me O Lord,
The serenity to accept
the things I cannot change;
the courage to change the things I should;
and the wisdom to know the difference.

Further Reading

Further Reading

ADAMS, Jay *Christian Living in the Home* (Nutley: Presbyterian and Reformed Publishing Co. 1972).

BROWN, Colin (Ed.) *Dictionary of New Testament Theology* – 'Divorce' I. H. Marshall, Vol. 1; 'Separate' (4) C. Brown, Vol. 3 – (Exeter: Paternoster Press 1978).

CAPPER, W. Melville and WILLIAMS, M. H. *Towards Christian Marriage* (Chicago: IVP 1958).

CHRISTENSON, Larry *The Christian Family* (Minneapolis: Bethany Fellowship 1970 & Eastbourne: Kingsway 1981).

COUSINS, Peter *Christianity and Sexual Liberation* (Exeter: Paternoster Press 1972).

DAHL, G. L. *Why Christian Marriages are Breaking Up* (Nashville: Nelson 1979).

DOBSON, James *Dare to Discipline* (Wheaton: Tyndale 1970 & Eastbourne: Kingsway 1971).

DUTY, Guy *Divorce and Remarriage* (Minneapolis: Bethany Fellowship 1967).

ELLISEN, Stanley A. *Divorce and Remarriage in the Church* (Grand Rapids: Zondervan 1977).

FISHER-HUNTER, W. *The Divorce Problem* (Waynesboro: Macneish 1952).

GALLOWAY, Dale *Dream a New Dream* (Wheaton, Tyndale 1975).

GANGEL, K. O. *The Family First* (Minneapolis: His International 1972).

GLADWYN, John *Happy Families* (Nottingham: Grove Books 1981).

GRAHAM, Mrs. Billy (*et al*) *The Family that Makes it* (Wheaton, Scripture Press 1971).

GREEN, Wendy *The Christian and Divorce* (Oxford: Mowbray 1981).

HENDRICKS, H. *Heaven help the home* (Wheaton: Scripture Press 1973).

HURDING, Roger *Restoring the Image* (Exeter: Paternoster Press 1980).

LANEY, J. Carl *The Divorce Myth* (Minneapolis: Bethany Fellowship 1981).

LEE, Helen *Christian Marriage* (Oxford: Mowbray 1977).

NARRAMORE, C. M. *How to succeed in family living* (Glendale: Gospel Light 1968).

PETERS, G. W. *Divorce and Remarriage* (Chicago: Moody 1970).

PETERSEN, J. A. (Ed.) *The Marriage Affair* (Wheaton: Tyndale 1971).

REID, Gavin *Starting Out Together* (London: Hodder 1981).

SMALL, D. H. *Design for Christian Marriage* (Westwood: Fleming H. Revell 1959).

SMALL, D. H. *The Right to Remarry* (Old Tappan: Fleming H. Revell 1975).

SMITH, H. I. *A Part of me is missing* (Irvine: Harvest House 1979).

SMOKE, Jim *Growing through Divorce* (Irvine: Harvest House 1976).

STOTT, J. R. W. *Divorce* (Downers Grove: IVP 1971 & London: Falcon 1972).

TENNEY, M. (Ed.) *Zondervan Pictorial Encyclopedia* (Grand Rapids: Zondervan 1975).

WARREN, Ann *Marriage in the Balance* (Eastbourne: Kingsway 1981).

WRIGHT, Norman *An Answer to Divorce* (Irvine: Harvest House 1977).

YOUNG, A. R. *By death or divorce – It hurts to lose* (Denver: Accent Books 1976).

ZUCK, Ray and GETZ, Gene A. *Ventures in Family Living* (Chicago: Moody 1970).

Scripture Index

Scripture Index